50 Poland Pizza Recipes for Home

By: Kelly Johnson

Table of Contents

- Pierogi Paradise Pizza
- Bigos Blast Pizza
- Golabki Delight Pizza
- Zurek Zest Pizza
- Kapusta Sensation Pizza
- Polskie Ogorki Extravaganza Pizza
- Krakow Fusion Pizza
- Mizeria Marvel Pizza
- Sernik Surprise Pizza
- Rosol Rendezvous Pizza
- Nalesniki Nirvana Pizza
- Wigilia Wonder Pizza
- Zapiekanka Bliss Pizza
- Silesian Streuselkuchen Supreme Pizza
- Cwikla Celebration Pizza
- Rogaliki Revel Pizza
- Polish Wedding Feast Pizza
- Ryba po Grecku Gourmet Pizza
- Jablecznik Joy Pizza
- Kluski Slaskie Sensation Pizza
- Placki Ziemniaczane Pleasure Pizza
- Oscypek Delicacy Pizza
- Kompot Carnival Pizza
- Paczki Perfection Pizza
- Ruskie Pierogi Extravaganza Pizza
- Makowiec Magic Pizza
- Zupa Grzybowa Goodness Pizza
- Pomidorowa Paradise Pizza
- Seromakowiec Sweetheart Pizza
- Kluski Kladzione Comfort Pizza
- Kapusta Kiszona Kick Pizza
- Lazanki Love Pizza
- Szarlotka Sensational Pizza
- Sernik na Zimno Zenith Pizza
- Kotlet Schabowy Supreme Pizza

- Zrazy Zest Pizza
- Mizeria z Papryka Pleasure Pizza
- Sernik Wiedenski Wonder Pizza
- Gołąbki z Indyka Elegance Pizza
- Placki Ziemniaczane z Lososiem Luxury Pizza
- Pieczen Rzymska Royal Pizza
- Krokiety Crisp Pizza
- Salceson Surprise Pizza
- Zupa Pomidorowa Pleasure Pizza
- Kluski z Makiem Marvel Pizza
- Zupa Fasolowa Flavor Pizza
- Kopytka Kiss Pizza
- Polish Honey Cake Delight Pizza
- Golonka Gourmet Pizza
- Twarog Treat Pizza

Pierogi Paradise Pizza

Ingredients:

- Pizza dough
- 1 cup mashed potatoes
- 1 cup shredded cheddar cheese
- 1/2 cup caramelized onions
- 1/2 cup cooked and crumbled bacon
- Sour cream (for drizzling)

Instructions:

Preheat your oven according to the pizza dough instructions.
Roll out the pizza dough on a floured surface to your desired thickness.
Spread the mashed potatoes evenly over the pizza dough, leaving a small border around the edges.
Sprinkle the shredded cheddar cheese over the mashed potatoes.
Scatter the caramelized onions and crumbled bacon over the cheese.
Bake the pizza in the preheated oven until the crust is golden and the cheese is melted and bubbly.
Remove from the oven and let it cool slightly.
Drizzle sour cream over the pizza before slicing.
Serve and enjoy your Pierogi Paradise Pizza!

Bigos Blast Pizza

Ingredients:

- Pizza dough
- 1 cup sauerkraut, drained
- 1 cup sliced kielbasa
- 1/2 cup sliced mushrooms
- 1 cup shredded mozzarella cheese
- 1 tablespoon olive oil
- Caraway seeds (for sprinkling)

Instructions:

Preheat your oven according to the pizza dough instructions.
Roll out the pizza dough on a floured surface to your desired thickness.
Spread sauerkraut evenly over the pizza dough.
Distribute sliced kielbasa and mushrooms over the sauerkraut.
Sprinkle shredded mozzarella cheese over the toppings.
Drizzle olive oil over the pizza.
Bake in the preheated oven until the crust is golden and the cheese is melted and bubbly.
Remove from the oven and sprinkle caraway seeds over the hot pizza.
Allow it to cool slightly before slicing.
Serve and savor the flavors of your Bigos Blast Pizza!

Golabki Delight Pizza

Ingredients:

- Pizza dough
- 1 cup ground pork, cooked
- 1 cup cooked rice
- 1 cup finely chopped cabbage leaves
- 1 cup tomato sauce
- 1 cup shredded mozzarella cheese
- Salt and pepper to taste

Instructions:

Preheat your oven according to the pizza dough instructions.
Roll out the pizza dough on a floured surface to your desired thickness.
In a bowl, mix cooked ground pork, cooked rice, chopped cabbage, salt, and pepper.
Spread tomato sauce evenly over the pizza dough.
Spoon the pork and rice mixture over the sauce.
Sprinkle shredded mozzarella cheese over the entire pizza.
Bake in the preheated oven until the crust is golden and the cheese is melted and bubbly.
Remove from the oven and let it cool for a few minutes.
Slice and serve your Golabki Delight Pizza, capturing the essence of traditional Golabki flavors in a pizza format!

Zurek Zest Pizza

Ingredients:

- Pizza dough
- 1 cup sliced kielbasa
- 2 hard-boiled eggs, sliced
- 1/2 cup sliced pickles
- 1/4 cup chopped fresh dill
- Sour cream (for drizzling)
- Salt and pepper to taste

Instructions:

Preheat your oven according to the pizza dough instructions.
Roll out the pizza dough on a floured surface to your desired thickness.
Spread sliced kielbasa evenly over the pizza dough.
Arrange slices of hard-boiled eggs and pickles on top of the kielbasa.
Season with salt and pepper to taste.
Bake in the preheated oven until the crust is golden, and the toppings are heated through.
Remove from the oven and sprinkle chopped fresh dill over the hot pizza.
Drizzle sour cream over the pizza before slicing.
Allow it to cool slightly, then serve your Zurek Zest Pizza, capturing the unique flavors of Zurek soup in pizza form!

Kapusta Sensation Pizza

Ingredients:

- Pizza dough
- 1 cup braised cabbage (finely chopped)
- 1 cup Polish sausage, sliced
- 1/2 cup red peppers, thinly sliced
- 1 cup provolone cheese, shredded
- Olive oil (for drizzling)
- Salt and pepper to taste

Instructions:

Preheat your oven according to the pizza dough instructions.
Roll out the pizza dough on a floured surface to your desired thickness.
Spread the finely chopped braised cabbage evenly over the pizza dough.
Distribute slices of Polish sausage and red pepper strips over the cabbage.
Sprinkle shredded provolone cheese over the entire pizza.
Drizzle olive oil over the toppings and season with salt and pepper to taste.
Bake in the preheated oven until the crust is golden and the cheese is melted and bubbly.
Remove from the oven and let it cool for a few minutes.
Slice and serve your Kapusta Sensation Pizza, a delightful blend of cabbage, sausage, and peppers on a pizza crust!

Polskie Ogorki Extravaganza Pizza

Ingredients:

- Pizza dough
- 1 cup dill pickles, thinly sliced
- 1 cup ham, diced
- 1/4 cup Dijon mustard
- 1 cup Swiss cheese, shredded
- Olive oil (for drizzling)

Instructions:

Preheat your oven according to the pizza dough instructions.
Roll out the pizza dough on a floured surface to your desired thickness.
Spread a thin layer of Dijon mustard evenly over the pizza dough.
Sprinkle diced ham and thinly sliced dill pickles over the mustard.
Evenly distribute shredded Swiss cheese over the entire pizza.
Drizzle a bit of olive oil over the toppings.
Bake in the preheated oven until the crust is golden, and the cheese is melted and bubbly.
Remove from the oven and let it cool for a few minutes.
Slice and serve your Polskie Ogorki Extravaganza Pizza, a flavorful combination of pickles, ham, and mustard on a pizza crust!

Krakow Fusion Pizza

Ingredients:

- Pizza dough
- 1 cup smoked cheese, shredded
- 1 cup Krakow-style sausage, thinly sliced
- 1/2 cup red bell peppers, diced
- 1/2 cup yellow onions, thinly sliced
- Olive oil (for drizzling)
- Fresh parsley (for garnish)

Instructions:

Preheat your oven according to the pizza dough instructions.
Roll out the pizza dough on a floured surface to your desired thickness.
Sprinkle the shredded smoked cheese evenly over the pizza dough.
Arrange slices of Krakow-style sausage, diced red bell peppers, and thinly sliced yellow onions on top of the cheese.
Drizzle a bit of olive oil over the toppings.
Bake in the preheated oven until the crust is golden, and the cheese is melted and bubbly.
Remove from the oven and let it cool for a few minutes.
Garnish with fresh parsley.
Slice and serve your Krakow Fusion Pizza, a delicious fusion of Krakow flavors on a pizza crust!

Mizeria Marvel Pizza

Ingredients:

- Pizza dough
- 1 cup cucumbers, thinly sliced
- 1/2 cup sour cream
- 1/4 cup fresh dill, chopped
- 1 cup smoked salmon, sliced
- Salt and pepper to taste
- Lemon wedges (for serving)

Instructions:

Preheat your oven according to the pizza dough instructions.
Roll out the pizza dough on a floured surface to your desired thickness.
Spread a thin layer of sour cream evenly over the pizza dough.
Arrange thinly sliced cucumbers over the sour cream.
Sprinkle chopped fresh dill over the cucumbers.
Place slices of smoked salmon on top of the cucumber and dill layer.
Season with salt and pepper to taste.
Bake in the preheated oven until the crust is golden, and the toppings are heated through.
Remove from the oven and let it cool for a few minutes.
Serve your Mizeria Marvel Pizza with lemon wedges on the side for an extra burst of flavor. Slice and enjoy!

Sernik Surprise Pizza

Ingredients:

- Pizza dough
- 1 cup sweetened cream cheese filling (sernik)
- 1/4 cup raisins
- 1/4 cup crushed graham crackers
- 1/4 cup powdered sugar
- 1 teaspoon vanilla extract

Instructions:

Preheat your oven according to the pizza dough instructions.
Roll out the pizza dough on a floured surface to your desired thickness.
Spread the sweetened cream cheese filling (sernik) evenly over the pizza dough.
Sprinkle raisins and crushed graham crackers over the cream cheese layer.
Drizzle vanilla extract evenly across the toppings.
Bake in the preheated oven until the crust is golden, and the toppings are heated through.
Remove from the oven and let it cool for a few minutes.
Dust the pizza with powdered sugar.
Slice and serve your Sernik Surprise Pizza, a delightful blend of sweetened cream cheese, raisins, and graham crackers on a pizza crust!

Rosol Rendezvous Pizza

Ingredients:

- Pizza dough
- 1 cup shredded cooked chicken
- Mixed root vegetables (carrots, parsnips, celery), finely diced
- Chicken broth reduction (for drizzling)
- Fresh parsley, chopped (for garnish)
- Salt and pepper to taste

Instructions:

Preheat your oven according to the pizza dough instructions.
Roll out the pizza dough on a floured surface to your desired thickness.
Spread the shredded cooked chicken evenly over the pizza dough.
Distribute the finely diced mixed root vegetables over the chicken.
Drizzle a reduced chicken broth evenly across the toppings.
Season with salt and pepper to taste.
Bake in the preheated oven until the crust is golden, and the toppings are heated through.
Remove from the oven and let it cool for a few minutes.
Garnish with freshly chopped parsley.
Slice and serve your Rosol Rendezvous Pizza, capturing the essence of Rosol (chicken broth) in a pizza format!

Nalesniki Nirvana Pizza

Ingredients:

- Crepe-style pizza crust
- Sweet cheese filling (cottage cheese, sugar, vanilla)
- Blueberry compote
- Powdered sugar (for dusting)

Instructions:

Prepare a crepe-style pizza crust or use pre-made crepes as the base.
Spread a generous layer of sweet cheese filling over the crepe crust.
Spoon blueberry compote over the sweet cheese filling.
Carefully fold or roll the crepe-style crust, creating a pizza shape.
Bake in the oven until the edges are golden, and the filling is warmed through.
Remove from the oven and let it cool for a few minutes.
Dust with powdered sugar before serving.
Slice and enjoy your Nalesniki Nirvana Pizza, a delightful combination of sweet cheese and blueberry flavors on a crepe crust!

Wigilia Wonder Pizza

Ingredients:

- Pizza dough
- Assorted fish (salmon, cod, herring), cooked and flaked
- Mushrooms, sautéed
- Beets, thinly sliced
- Horseradish cream sauce
- Fresh dill, chopped (for garnish)

Instructions:

Preheat your oven according to the pizza dough instructions.
Roll out the pizza dough on a floured surface to your desired thickness.
Spread the flaked cooked fish evenly over the pizza dough.
Scatter sautéed mushrooms and thinly sliced beets over the fish.
Drizzle horseradish cream sauce evenly across the toppings.
Bake in the preheated oven until the crust is golden, and the toppings are heated through.
Remove from the oven and let it cool for a few minutes.
Garnish with freshly chopped dill.
Slice and serve your Wigilia Wonder Pizza, a festive pizza inspired by traditional Wigilia (Christmas Eve) flavors!

Zapiekanka Bliss Pizza

Ingredients:

- French baguette or Italian bread (as pizza crust)
- 2 cups mushrooms, sliced
- 1 large onion, thinly sliced
- 2 cloves garlic, minced
- 1 cup ham, diced
- 2 cups mozzarella cheese, shredded
- Ketchup (for drizzling)
- Mustard (for drizzling)
- Fresh chives, chopped (for garnish)

Instructions:

Preheat your oven according to the bread instructions.
Slice the baguette or Italian bread in half lengthwise to create the pizza crust.
In a pan, sauté mushrooms, onions, and minced garlic until softened.
Spread the sautéed mushroom mixture evenly over the bread.
Sprinkle diced ham over the mushrooms and onions.
Generously cover the pizza with shredded mozzarella cheese.
Drizzle ketchup and mustard over the toppings.
Bake in the preheated oven until the cheese is melted, bubbly, and the crust is golden.
Remove from the oven and let it cool for a few minutes.
Garnish with freshly chopped chives.
Slice and serve your Zapiekanka Bliss Pizza, a delicious twist on the classic Polish street food!

Silesian Streuselkuchen Supreme Pizza

Ingredients:

- Pizza dough
- Streusel topping (flour, sugar, butter, cinnamon)
- 1 cup sweetened cream cheese
- 1/2 cup raisins
- Powdered sugar (for dusting)

Instructions:

Preheat your oven according to the pizza dough instructions.
Roll out the pizza dough on a floured surface to your desired thickness.
In a bowl, mix together flour, sugar, butter, and cinnamon to create the streusel topping.
Spread the sweetened cream cheese evenly over the pizza dough.
Sprinkle the streusel topping generously over the cream cheese.
Scatter raisins over the streusel topping.
Bake in the preheated oven until the crust is golden and the streusel is crisp.
Remove from the oven and let it cool for a few minutes.
Dust with powdered sugar before serving.
Slice and serve your Silesian Streuselkuchen Supreme Pizza, a delightful fusion of pizza and traditional German streuselkuchen flavors!

Cwikla Celebration Pizza

Ingredients:

- Pizza dough
- 1 cup grated horseradish (cwikla)
- 1 cup beets, cooked and thinly sliced
- 1/2 cup sour cream
- 1/4 cup chopped fresh dill
- Smoked salmon, thinly sliced
- Lemon wedges (for serving)

Instructions:

Preheat your oven according to the pizza dough instructions.
Roll out the pizza dough on a floured surface to your desired thickness.
Spread the grated horseradish (cwikla) evenly over the pizza dough.
Arrange thinly sliced beets over the horseradish.
Drizzle sour cream over the beets and horseradish.
Scatter chopped fresh dill over the entire pizza.
Place thinly sliced smoked salmon on top of the pizza.
Bake in the preheated oven until the crust is golden, and the toppings are heated through.
Remove from the oven and let it cool for a few minutes.
Serve your Cwikla Celebration Pizza with lemon wedges on the side for added zest.
Slice and enjoy this festive pizza inspired by the flavors of cwikla, a traditional Polish condiment!

Rogaliki Revel Pizza

Ingredients:

- Pizza dough
- 1 cup apricot jam
- 1/2 cup ground walnuts
- 1/4 cup powdered sugar
- 1 teaspoon cinnamon
- 1 egg (for egg wash)
- Sliced almonds (for garnish)

Instructions:

Preheat your oven according to the pizza dough instructions.
Roll out the pizza dough on a floured surface to your desired thickness.
Spread apricot jam evenly over the pizza dough, leaving a small border around the edges.
In a bowl, mix ground walnuts, powdered sugar, and cinnamon. Sprinkle this mixture over the apricot jam.
Carefully roll the pizza dough into a log, creating a rolled pastry-like shape.
Beat the egg and brush it over the rolled pizza dough for a golden finish.
Bake in the preheated oven until the crust is golden and the filling is set.
Remove from the oven and let it cool for a few minutes.
Garnish with sliced almonds.
Slice and serve your Rogaliki Revel Pizza, a delightful pizza inspired by the flavors of traditional Polish rogaliki pastries!

Polish Wedding Feast Pizza

Ingredients:

- Pizza dough
- 1 cup cooked chicken, shredded
- 1 cup sautéed mushrooms
- 1/2 cup bell peppers, thinly sliced
- 1/2 cup onions, caramelized
- 1 cup sour cream
- Fresh dill, chopped
- Salt and pepper to taste

Instructions:

Preheat your oven according to the pizza dough instructions.
Roll out the pizza dough on a floured surface to your desired thickness.
Spread a layer of sour cream evenly over the pizza dough.
Distribute shredded chicken, sautéed mushrooms, thinly sliced bell peppers, and caramelized onions over the sour cream.
Sprinkle chopped fresh dill over the entire pizza.
Season with salt and pepper to taste.
Bake in the preheated oven until the crust is golden, and the toppings are heated through.
Remove from the oven and let it cool for a few minutes.
Slice and serve your Polish Wedding Feast Pizza, capturing the diverse and savory flavors of a traditional Polish wedding feast on a pizza crust!

Ryba po Grecku Gourmet Pizza

Ingredients:

- Pizza dough
- 1 cup flaked fish (salmon, cod, or haddock)
- 1 cup Greek-style tomato sauce
- 1/2 cup black olives, sliced
- 1/2 cup red onions, thinly sliced
- Feta cheese, crumbled
- Fresh parsley, chopped
- Lemon wedges (for serving)

Instructions:

Preheat your oven according to the pizza dough instructions.
Roll out the pizza dough on a floured surface to your desired thickness.
Spread a layer of Greek-style tomato sauce evenly over the pizza dough.
Distribute the flaked fish over the sauce.
Scatter sliced black olives and thinly sliced red onions over the fish.
Crumble feta cheese generously over the entire pizza.
Bake in the preheated oven until the crust is golden, and the toppings are heated through.
Remove from the oven and sprinkle freshly chopped parsley over the hot pizza.
Serve with lemon wedges on the side for an extra burst of flavor.
Slice and enjoy your Ryba po Grecku Gourmet Pizza, a fusion of Greek and Polish flavors on a pizza crust!

Jablecznik Joy Pizza

Ingredients:

- Pizza dough
- 2 cups apples, thinly sliced
- 1/4 cup brown sugar
- 1 teaspoon ground cinnamon
- 1/4 cup raisins
- Streusel topping (flour, sugar, butter, cinnamon)
- Vanilla ice cream (for serving, optional)

Instructions:

Preheat your oven according to the pizza dough instructions.
Roll out the pizza dough on a floured surface to your desired thickness.
In a bowl, mix thinly sliced apples, brown sugar, ground cinnamon, and raisins.
Spread the apple mixture evenly over the pizza dough.
In a separate bowl, combine flour, sugar, butter, and cinnamon to create the streusel topping. Sprinkle this mixture generously over the apples.
Bake in the preheated oven until the crust is golden, and the streusel is crisp.
Remove from the oven and let it cool for a few minutes.
Optionally, serve with a scoop of vanilla ice cream on top.
Slice and enjoy your Jablecznik Joy Pizza, a delightful apple and streusel dessert on a pizza crust!

Kluski Slaskie Sensation Pizza

Ingredients:

- Pizza dough
- 1 cup potato dumplings (Kluski Slaskie), sliced
- 1/2 cup bacon bits
- 1/2 cup caramelized onions
- 1 cup sour cream
- Chives, chopped (for garnish)
- Salt and pepper to taste

Instructions:

Preheat your oven according to the pizza dough instructions.
Roll out the pizza dough on a floured surface to your desired thickness.
Spread a layer of sour cream evenly over the pizza dough.
Distribute sliced Kluski Slaskie (potato dumplings) over the sour cream.
Sprinkle bacon bits and caramelized onions over the potato dumplings.
Season with salt and pepper to taste.
Bake in the preheated oven until the crust is golden, and the toppings are heated through.
Remove from the oven and let it cool for a few minutes.
Garnish with chopped chives.
Slice and serve your Kluski Slaskie Sensation Pizza, a unique and delightful twist on traditional Polish dumplings on a pizza crust!

Placki Ziemniaczane Pleasure Pizza

Ingredients:

- Pizza dough
- 1 cup Placki Ziemniaczane (potato pancakes), shredded
- 1/2 cup sour cream
- 1/4 cup applesauce
- 1/4 cup chives, chopped
- Salt and pepper to taste

Instructions:

Preheat your oven according to the pizza dough instructions.
Roll out the pizza dough on a floured surface to your desired thickness.
Spread a layer of sour cream evenly over the pizza dough.
Distribute shredded Placki Ziemniaczane (potato pancakes) over the sour cream.
Season with salt and pepper to taste.
Drizzle applesauce over the potato pancakes.
Bake in the preheated oven until the crust is golden, and the toppings are heated through.
Remove from the oven and let it cool for a few minutes.
Sprinkle chopped chives over the hot pizza.
Slice and serve your Placki Ziemniaczane Pleasure Pizza, a delicious combination of potato pancakes, sour cream, and applesauce on a pizza crust!

Oscypek Delicacy Pizza

Ingredients:

- Pizza dough
- 1 cup Oscypek cheese, grated
- 1/2 cup cranberry sauce
- 1/4 cup honey
- 1/4 cup walnuts, chopped
- Fresh thyme leaves (for garnish)

Instructions:

Preheat your oven according to the pizza dough instructions.
Roll out the pizza dough on a floured surface to your desired thickness.
Spread the grated Oscypek cheese evenly over the pizza dough.
Spoon dollops of cranberry sauce over the cheese.
Drizzle honey across the toppings.
Sprinkle chopped walnuts over the entire pizza.
Bake in the preheated oven until the crust is golden, and the cheese is melted and bubbly.
Remove from the oven and let it cool for a few minutes.
Garnish with fresh thyme leaves.
Slice and serve your Oscypek Delicacy Pizza, a unique and delightful blend of Oscypek cheese, cranberry sauce, and honey on a pizza crust!

Kompot Carnival Pizza

Ingredients:

- Pizza dough
- 1 cup mixed dried fruits (apricots, prunes, raisins)
- 1 cup fruit compote (kompot)
- 1/2 cup cream cheese
- 1/4 cup powdered sugar
- 1/4 cup slivered almonds (for topping)

Instructions:

Preheat your oven according to the pizza dough instructions.

Roll out the pizza dough on a floured surface to your desired thickness.

In a bowl, mix the cream cheese and powdered sugar until smooth. Spread this mixture evenly over the pizza dough.

Arrange mixed dried fruits over the cream cheese layer.

Pour fruit compote (kompot) over the dried fruits.

Bake in the preheated oven until the crust is golden, and the toppings are heated through.

Remove from the oven and let it cool for a few minutes.

Sprinkle slivered almonds over the hot pizza.

Slice and serve your Kompot Carnival Pizza, a delightful celebration of mixed dried fruits and fruit compote on a pizza crust!

Paczki Perfection Pizza

Ingredients:

- Pizza dough
- 1 cup paczki (Polish doughnuts), sliced
- 1/2 cup raspberry jam
- 1/4 cup powdered sugar
- 1/4 cup chocolate ganache (optional)
- Fresh mint leaves (for garnish)

Instructions:

Preheat your oven according to the pizza dough instructions.
Roll out the pizza dough on a floured surface to your desired thickness.
Spread a thin layer of raspberry jam evenly over the pizza dough.
Arrange sliced paczki over the raspberry jam.
Bake in the preheated oven until the crust is golden, and the paczki are heated through.
If desired, drizzle chocolate ganache over the paczki.
Remove from the oven and let it cool for a few minutes.
Dust the pizza with powdered sugar.
Garnish with fresh mint leaves.
Slice and serve your Paczki Perfection Pizza, a sweet and indulgent treat inspired by traditional Polish doughnuts on a pizza crust!

Ruskie Pierogi Extravaganza Pizza

Ingredients:

- Pizza dough
- 1 cup mashed potatoes
- 1/2 cup farmer's cheese
- 1/2 cup caramelized onions
- 1/4 cup cooked and crumbled bacon
- Sour cream (for drizzling)
- Chives, chopped (for garnish)
- Salt and pepper to taste

Instructions:

Preheat your oven according to the pizza dough instructions.
Roll out the pizza dough on a floured surface to your desired thickness.
Spread a layer of mashed potatoes evenly over the pizza dough.
Crumble farmer's cheese over the mashed potatoes.
Scatter caramelized onions and cooked, crumbled bacon over the cheese and potatoes.
Season with salt and pepper to taste.
Bake in the preheated oven until the crust is golden, and the toppings are heated through.
Remove from the oven and let it cool for a few minutes.
Drizzle sour cream over the hot pizza.
Garnish with chopped chives.
Slice and serve your Ruskie Pierogi Extravaganza Pizza, a creative twist on traditional pierogi flavors on a pizza crust!

Makowiec Magic Pizza

Ingredients:

- Pizza dough
- 1 cup poppy seed filling (Makowiec filling)
- 1/2 cup honey
- 1/4 cup chopped walnuts
- 1/4 cup raisins
- Powdered sugar (for dusting)

Instructions:

Preheat your oven according to the pizza dough instructions.
Roll out the pizza dough on a floured surface to your desired thickness.
Spread a generous layer of poppy seed filling (Makowiec filling) evenly over the pizza dough.
Drizzle honey over the poppy seed filling.
Sprinkle chopped walnuts and raisins over the entire pizza.
Bake in the preheated oven until the crust is golden, and the toppings are heated through.
Remove from the oven and let it cool for a few minutes.
Dust with powdered sugar before serving.
Slice and enjoy your Makowiec Magic Pizza, a delightful fusion of poppy seed and honey flavors on a pizza crust!

Zupa Grzybowa Goodness Pizza

Ingredients:

- Pizza dough
- 1 cup mushroom soup (Zupa Grzybowa), cooked and thickened
- 1 cup mixed mushrooms, sliced (such as cremini, shiitake, or button mushrooms)
- 1/2 cup caramelized onions
- 1 cup mozzarella cheese, shredded
- Fresh thyme leaves (for garnish)
- Truffle oil (for drizzling, optional)

Instructions:

Preheat your oven according to the pizza dough instructions.
Roll out the pizza dough on a floured surface to your desired thickness.
Spread a layer of the cooked and thickened mushroom soup (Zupa Grzybowa) evenly over the pizza dough.
Distribute sliced mixed mushrooms and caramelized onions over the soup.
Sprinkle shredded mozzarella cheese over the entire pizza.
Bake in the preheated oven until the crust is golden, and the cheese is melted and bubbly.
Remove from the oven and let it cool for a few minutes.
Garnish with fresh thyme leaves.
Optionally, drizzle truffle oil over the hot pizza.
Slice and serve your Zupa Grzybowa Goodness Pizza, a unique and savory pizza inspired by Polish mushroom soup!

Pomidorowa Paradise Pizza

Ingredients:

- Pizza dough
- 1 cup tomato sauce
- 1/2 cup cherry tomatoes, halved
- 1/4 cup sun-dried tomatoes, sliced
- 1 cup fresh mozzarella, torn into pieces
- Fresh basil leaves (for garnish)
- Olive oil (for drizzling)
- Salt and pepper to taste

Instructions:

Preheat your oven according to the pizza dough instructions.
Roll out the pizza dough on a floured surface to your desired thickness.
Spread a layer of tomato sauce evenly over the pizza dough.
Arrange halved cherry tomatoes and sliced sun-dried tomatoes over the sauce.
Distribute torn pieces of fresh mozzarella across the pizza.
Season with salt and pepper to taste.
Bake in the preheated oven until the crust is golden, and the cheese is melted and bubbly.
Remove from the oven and let it cool for a few minutes.
Garnish with fresh basil leaves.
Drizzle olive oil over the hot pizza before slicing.
Slice and enjoy your Pomidorowa Paradise Pizza, a delightful fusion of pizza with the flavors of Polish tomato soup!

Seromakowiec Sweetheart Pizza

Ingredients:

- Pizza dough
- 1 cup sweetened farmer's cheese filling (seromakowiec)
- 1/4 cup apricot preserves
- 1/4 cup chopped walnuts
- 1/4 cup raisins
- Powdered sugar (for dusting)

Instructions:

Preheat your oven according to the pizza dough instructions.
Roll out the pizza dough on a floured surface to your desired thickness.
Spread the sweetened farmer's cheese filling (seromakowiec) evenly over the pizza dough.
Spoon apricot preserves over the cheese filling.
Sprinkle chopped walnuts and raisins over the entire pizza.
Bake in the preheated oven until the crust is golden, and the toppings are heated through.
Remove from the oven and let it cool for a few minutes.
Dust with powdered sugar before serving.
Slice and enjoy your Seromakowiec Sweetheart Pizza, a sweet and delicious treat inspired by the traditional Polish dessert!

Kluski Kladzione Comfort Pizza

Ingredients:

- Pizza dough
- 1 cup Kluski Kładzione (drop noodles), cooked
- 1/2 cup butter, melted
- 1/4 cup breadcrumbs
- 1/4 cup Parmesan cheese, grated
- Fresh parsley, chopped (for garnish)
- Salt and pepper to taste

Instructions:

Preheat your oven according to the pizza dough instructions.
Roll out the pizza dough on a floured surface to your desired thickness.
In a bowl, toss the cooked Kluski Kładzione with melted butter until well-coated.
Spread the buttered Kluski Kładzione evenly over the pizza dough.
In a small bowl, mix breadcrumbs and Parmesan cheese. Sprinkle this mixture over the noodles.
Season with salt and pepper to taste.
Bake in the preheated oven until the crust is golden, and the toppings are heated through.
Remove from the oven and let it cool for a few minutes.
Garnish with chopped fresh parsley.
Slice and serve your Kluski Kładzione Comfort Pizza, a comforting and unique pizza inspired by traditional Polish drop noodles!

Kapusta Kiszona Kick Pizza

Ingredients:

- Pizza dough
- 1 cup sauerkraut (kapusta kiszona), drained and squeezed
- 1 cup kielbasa, thinly sliced
- 1/2 cup shredded Polish smoked cheese
- 1/4 cup Dijon mustard
- Caraway seeds (for sprinkling)
- Fresh parsley, chopped (for garnish)

Instructions:

Preheat your oven according to the pizza dough instructions.
Roll out the pizza dough on a floured surface to your desired thickness.
Spread a layer of Dijon mustard evenly over the pizza dough.
Distribute the drained and squeezed sauerkraut over the mustard.
Arrange thinly sliced kielbasa over the sauerkraut.
Sprinkle shredded Polish smoked cheese over the entire pizza.
Sprinkle caraway seeds over the toppings.
Bake in the preheated oven until the crust is golden, and the cheese is melted and bubbly.
Remove from the oven and let it cool for a few minutes.
Garnish with chopped fresh parsley.
Slice and serve your Kapusta Kiszona Kick Pizza, a flavor-packed pizza inspired by the tangy goodness of sauerkraut and kielbasa!

Lazanki Love Pizza

Ingredients:

- Pizza dough
- 1 cup cooked egg noodles (lazanki)
- 1/2 cup caramelized onions
- 1/2 cup cooked cabbage, chopped
- 1 cup Polish sausage, sliced
- 1/2 cup sour cream
- Fresh dill, chopped (for garnish)
- Salt and pepper to taste

Instructions:

Preheat your oven according to the pizza dough instructions.
Roll out the pizza dough on a floured surface to your desired thickness.
Spread a layer of sour cream evenly over the pizza dough.
Distribute cooked egg noodles over the sour cream.
Scatter caramelized onions, chopped cooked cabbage, and sliced Polish sausage over the noodles.
Season with salt and pepper to taste.
Bake in the preheated oven until the crust is golden, and the toppings are heated through.
Remove from the oven and let it cool for a few minutes.
Garnish with chopped fresh dill.
Slice and serve your Lazanki Love Pizza, a comforting blend of egg noodles, cabbage, and sausage on a pizza crust!

Szarlotka Sensational Pizza

Ingredients:

- Pizza dough
- 2 cups apples, thinly sliced
- 1/4 cup brown sugar
- 1 teaspoon ground cinnamon
- Streusel topping (flour, sugar, butter, cinnamon)
- Caramel sauce (for drizzling)
- Vanilla ice cream (for serving, optional)

Instructions:

Preheat your oven according to the pizza dough instructions.
Roll out the pizza dough on a floured surface to your desired thickness.
In a bowl, mix thinly sliced apples, brown sugar, and ground cinnamon.
Spread the apple mixture evenly over the pizza dough.
In a separate bowl, combine flour, sugar, butter, and cinnamon to create the streusel topping. Sprinkle this mixture generously over the apples.
Bake in the preheated oven until the crust is golden, and the streusel is crisp.
Remove from the oven and let it cool for a few minutes.
Drizzle caramel sauce over the hot pizza.
Optionally, serve with a scoop of vanilla ice cream on top.
Slice and enjoy your Szarlotka Sensational Pizza, a delicious apple streusel dessert on a pizza crust!

Sernik na Zimno Zenith Pizza

Ingredients:

- Pizza dough
- 1 cup no-bake cheesecake filling (Sernik na Zimno)
- 1/4 cup fruit preserves (your choice)
- Fresh berries (strawberries, blueberries, raspberries)
- Mint leaves (for garnish)
- Powdered sugar (for dusting)

Instructions:

Preheat your oven according to the pizza dough instructions.
Roll out the pizza dough on a floured surface to your desired thickness.
Spread a layer of the no-bake cheesecake filling (Sernik na Zimno) evenly over the pizza dough.
Dollop fruit preserves over the cheesecake filling.
Scatter fresh berries over the entire pizza.
Bake in the preheated oven until the crust is golden.
Remove from the oven and let it cool for a few minutes.
Garnish with mint leaves.
Dust with powdered sugar before serving.
Slice and serve your Sernik na Zimno Zenith Pizza, a refreshing and delightful no-bake cheesecake-inspired dessert on a pizza crust!

Kotlet Schabowy Supreme Pizza

Ingredients:

- Pizza dough
- 1 cup breaded and fried pork cutlet (kotlet schabowy), thinly sliced
- 1/2 cup mashed potatoes
- 1/4 cup peas
- 1/4 cup carrots, diced and cooked
- 1/2 cup cheddar cheese, shredded
- 1/4 cup sour cream
- Fresh parsley, chopped (for garnish)
- Salt and pepper to taste

Instructions:

Preheat your oven according to the pizza dough instructions.
Roll out the pizza dough on a floured surface to your desired thickness.
Spread a layer of mashed potatoes evenly over the pizza dough.
Arrange thinly sliced breaded and fried pork cutlet (kotlet schabowy) over the mashed potatoes.
Distribute cooked peas and diced carrots over the pork cutlet.
Sprinkle shredded cheddar cheese over the entire pizza.
Season with salt and pepper to taste.
Bake in the preheated oven until the crust is golden, and the toppings are heated through.
Remove from the oven and let it cool for a few minutes.
Drizzle sour cream over the hot pizza.
Garnish with chopped fresh parsley.
Slice and serve your Kotlet Schabowy Supreme Pizza, a satisfying combination of pork cutlet, mashed potatoes, and vegetables on a pizza crust!

Mizeria z Papryka Pleasure Pizza

Ingredients:

- Pizza dough
- 1 cup cucumber, thinly sliced
- 1/2 cup red bell pepper, thinly sliced
- 1/4 cup red onion, thinly sliced
- 1/2 cup sour cream
- 1 tablespoon white wine vinegar
- Fresh dill, chopped
- Salt and pepper to taste

Instructions:

Preheat your oven according to the pizza dough instructions.
Roll out the pizza dough on a floured surface to your desired thickness.
In a bowl, mix together cucumber, red bell pepper, and red onion slices.
In a separate bowl, whisk together sour cream and white wine vinegar. Season with salt and pepper.
Spread a layer of the sour cream mixture evenly over the pizza dough.
Distribute the mixed cucumber, red bell pepper, and red onion slices over the sour cream layer.
Bake in the preheated oven until the crust is golden, and the toppings are heated through.
Remove from the oven and let it cool for a few minutes.
Sprinkle chopped fresh dill over the hot pizza.
Slice and serve your Mizeria z Papryką Pleasure Pizza, a refreshing and delightful pizza inspired by the Polish cucumber salad with a twist of red bell pepper!

Zrazy Zest Pizza

Ingredients:

- Pizza dough
- 1 cup beef roulades (zrazy), cooked and sliced
- 1/2 cup caramelized onions
- 1/2 cup sautéed mushrooms
- 1 cup mozzarella cheese, shredded
- 1/4 cup Dijon mustard
- Fresh parsley, chopped (for garnish)
- Salt and pepper to taste

Instructions:

Preheat your oven according to the pizza dough instructions.
Roll out the pizza dough on a floured surface to your desired thickness.
Spread a layer of Dijon mustard evenly over the pizza dough.
Distribute sliced beef roulades (zrazy) over the mustard.
Scatter caramelized onions and sautéed mushrooms over the beef.
Sprinkle shredded mozzarella cheese over the entire pizza.
Season with salt and pepper to taste.
Bake in the preheated oven until the crust is golden, and the cheese is melted and bubbly.
Remove from the oven and let it cool for a few minutes.
Garnish with chopped fresh parsley.
Slice and serve your Zrazy Zest Pizza, a flavorful pizza inspired by the classic Polish beef roulades!

Sernik Wiedenski Wonder Pizza

Ingredients:

- Pizza dough
- 1 cup Viennese cheesecake filling (Sernik Wiedeński)
- 1/4 cup raspberry jam
- 1/4 cup chocolate chips
- 1/4 cup slivered almonds
- Powdered sugar (for dusting)

Instructions:

Preheat your oven according to the pizza dough instructions.
Roll out the pizza dough on a floured surface to your desired thickness.
Spread a layer of Viennese cheesecake filling (Sernik Wiedeński) evenly over the pizza dough.
Dollop raspberry jam over the cheesecake filling.
Sprinkle chocolate chips and slivered almonds over the entire pizza.
Bake in the preheated oven until the crust is golden, and the toppings are heated through.
Remove from the oven and let it cool for a few minutes.
Dust with powdered sugar before serving.
Slice and enjoy your Sernik Wiedeński Wonder Pizza, a delicious combination of Viennese cheesecake, raspberry, chocolate, and almonds on a pizza crust!

Gołąbki z Indyka Elegance Pizza

Ingredients:

- Pizza dough
- 1 cup ground turkey or turkey sausage, cooked and seasoned
- 1/2 cup cooked rice
- 1/2 cup tomato sauce
- 1/4 cup sauerkraut
- 1 cup mozzarella cheese, shredded
- Fresh parsley, chopped (for garnish)
- Salt and pepper to taste

Instructions:

Preheat your oven according to the pizza dough instructions.
Roll out the pizza dough on a floured surface to your desired thickness.
Spread a layer of tomato sauce evenly over the pizza dough.
In a bowl, mix together cooked and seasoned ground turkey (or turkey sausage) with cooked rice.
Distribute the turkey and rice mixture over the tomato sauce.
Sprinkle sauerkraut over the turkey mixture.
Sprinkle shredded mozzarella cheese over the entire pizza.
Season with salt and pepper to taste.
Bake in the preheated oven until the crust is golden, and the cheese is melted and bubbly.
Remove from the oven and let it cool for a few minutes.
Garnish with chopped fresh parsley.
Slice and serve your Gołąbki z Indyka Elegance Pizza, a pizza inspired by the flavors of traditional Polish turkey-stuffed cabbage rolls!

Placki Ziemniaczane z Lososiem Luxury Pizza

Ingredients:

- Pizza dough
- 1 cup Potato pancakes (Placki Ziemniaczane), shredded
- 1/2 cup cream cheese
- 1/4 cup smoked salmon, thinly sliced
- 1/4 cup red onion, thinly sliced
- Capers (for garnish)
- Fresh dill, chopped (for garnish)
- Lemon wedges (for serving)

Instructions:

Preheat your oven according to the pizza dough instructions.
Roll out the pizza dough on a floured surface to your desired thickness.
Spread a layer of cream cheese evenly over the pizza dough.
Distribute shredded potato pancakes (Placki Ziemniaczane) over the cream cheese.
Arrange thinly sliced smoked salmon and red onion over the potato pancakes.
Sprinkle capers over the entire pizza.
Bake in the preheated oven until the crust is golden, and the toppings are heated through.
Remove from the oven and let it cool for a few minutes.
Garnish with chopped fresh dill.
Serve with lemon wedges on the side for added flavor.
Slice and enjoy your Placki Ziemniaczane z Łososiem Luxury Pizza, a luxurious pizza featuring the classic Polish potato pancakes with smoked salmon!

Pieczen Rzymska Royal Pizza

Ingredients:

- Pizza dough
- 1 cup sliced roast beef (Pieczeń Rzymska)
- 1/2 cup caramelized onions
- 1/2 cup roasted red peppers, sliced
- 1 cup provolone cheese, shredded
- 1/4 cup mayonnaise
- Fresh arugula (for garnish)
- Balsamic glaze (for drizzling)
- Salt and pepper to taste

Instructions:

Preheat your oven according to the pizza dough instructions.
Roll out the pizza dough on a floured surface to your desired thickness.
Spread a thin layer of mayonnaise evenly over the pizza dough.
Distribute sliced roast beef over the mayonnaise layer.
Scatter caramelized onions and sliced roasted red peppers over the beef.
Sprinkle shredded provolone cheese over the entire pizza.
Season with salt and pepper to taste.
Bake in the preheated oven until the crust is golden, and the cheese is melted and bubbly.
Remove from the oven and let it cool for a few minutes.
Garnish with fresh arugula.
Drizzle balsamic glaze over the hot pizza before slicing.
Slice and serve your Pieczeń Rzymska Royal Pizza, a regal combination of roast beef, caramelized onions, and provolone cheese on a pizza crust!

Krokiety Crisp Pizza

Ingredients:

- Pizza dough
- 1 cup krokiety (Polish croquettes), sliced
- 1/2 cup sautéed mushrooms
- 1/2 cup ham, diced
- 1 cup Swiss cheese, shredded
- 1/4 cup Dijon mustard
- Fresh parsley, chopped (for garnish)
- Salt and pepper to taste

Instructions:

Preheat your oven according to the pizza dough instructions.
Roll out the pizza dough on a floured surface to your desired thickness.
Spread a layer of Dijon mustard evenly over the pizza dough.
Distribute sliced krokiety over the mustard.
Scatter sautéed mushrooms and diced ham over the krokiety.
Sprinkle shredded Swiss cheese over the entire pizza.
Season with salt and pepper to taste.
Bake in the preheated oven until the crust is golden, and the cheese is melted and bubbly.
Remove from the oven and let it cool for a few minutes.
Garnish with chopped fresh parsley.
Slice and serve your Krokiety Crisp Pizza, a unique and delicious pizza inspired by the flavors of Polish croquettes!

Salceson Surprise Pizza

Ingredients:

- Pizza dough
- 1 cup salceson (Polish headcheese), thinly sliced
- 1/2 cup pickles, sliced
- 1/4 cup yellow mustard
- 1 cup mozzarella cheese, shredded
- Fresh dill, chopped (for garnish)
- Salt and pepper to taste

Instructions:

Preheat your oven according to the pizza dough instructions.
Roll out the pizza dough on a floured surface to your desired thickness.
Spread a layer of yellow mustard evenly over the pizza dough.
Distribute thinly sliced salceson over the mustard.
Scatter sliced pickles over the salceson.
Sprinkle shredded mozzarella cheese over the entire pizza.
Season with salt and pepper to taste.
Bake in the preheated oven until the crust is golden, and the cheese is melted and bubbly.
Remove from the oven and let it cool for a few minutes.
Garnish with chopped fresh dill.
Slice and serve your Salceson Surprise Pizza, a unique and flavorful pizza inspired by the traditional Polish headcheese!

Zupa Pomidorowa Pleasure Pizza

Ingredients:

- Pizza dough
- 1 cup tomato soup (Zupa Pomidorowa), cooked and thickened
- 1/2 cup fresh tomatoes, diced
- 1/4 cup red onion, thinly sliced
- 1 cup mozzarella cheese, shredded
- Fresh basil leaves (for garnish)
- Olive oil (for drizzling)
- Salt and pepper to taste

Instructions:

Preheat your oven according to the pizza dough instructions.
Roll out the pizza dough on a floured surface to your desired thickness.
Spread a layer of the cooked and thickened tomato soup (Zupa Pomidorowa) evenly over the pizza dough.
Distribute diced fresh tomatoes and thinly sliced red onion over the soup.
Sprinkle shredded mozzarella cheese over the entire pizza.
Season with salt and pepper to taste.
Bake in the preheated oven until the crust is golden, and the cheese is melted and bubbly.
Remove from the oven and let it cool for a few minutes.
Garnish with fresh basil leaves.
Drizzle olive oil over the hot pizza before slicing.
Slice and serve your Zupa Pomidorowa Pleasure Pizza, a delightful fusion of pizza with the flavors of Polish tomato soup!

Kluski z Makiem Marvel Pizza

Ingredients:

- Pizza dough
- 1 cup cooked egg noodles or dumplings (kluski)
- 1/2 cup poppy seed filling (mak)
- 1/4 cup honey
- 1/4 cup walnuts, chopped
- Powdered sugar (for dusting)

Instructions:

Preheat your oven according to the pizza dough instructions.
Roll out the pizza dough on a floured surface to your desired thickness.
Spread a layer of poppy seed filling (mak) evenly over the pizza dough.
Distribute cooked egg noodles or dumplings (kluski) over the poppy seed filling.
Drizzle honey over the noodles.
Sprinkle chopped walnuts over the entire pizza.
Bake in the preheated oven until the crust is golden, and the toppings are heated through.
Remove from the oven and let it cool for a few minutes.
Dust with powdered sugar before serving.
Slice and enjoy your Kluski z Makiem Marvel Pizza, a sweet and nutty delight inspired by traditional Polish poppy seed noodles!

Zupa Fasolowa Flavor Pizza

Ingredients:

- Pizza dough
- 1 cup cooked white beans (fasola)
- 1/2 cup kielbasa, sliced
- 1/4 cup onion, finely chopped
- 1/4 cup tomato sauce
- 1 cup mozzarella cheese, shredded
- Fresh parsley, chopped (for garnish)
- Olive oil (for drizzling)
- Salt and pepper to taste

Instructions:

Preheat your oven according to the pizza dough instructions.
Roll out the pizza dough on a floured surface to your desired thickness.
Spread a layer of tomato sauce evenly over the pizza dough.
Distribute cooked white beans over the tomato sauce.
Scatter sliced kielbasa and finely chopped onion over the beans.
Sprinkle shredded mozzarella cheese over the entire pizza.
Season with salt and pepper to taste.
Bake in the preheated oven until the crust is golden, and the cheese is melted and bubbly.
Remove from the oven and let it cool for a few minutes.
Garnish with chopped fresh parsley.
Drizzle olive oil over the hot pizza before slicing.
Slice and serve your Zupa Fasolowa Flavor Pizza, a unique pizza inspired by the rich flavors of Polish bean soup!

Kopytka Kiss Pizza

Ingredients:

- Pizza dough
- 1 cup cooked kopytka (Polish potato dumplings), diced
- 1/2 cup bacon, cooked and crumbled
- 1/4 cup caramelized onions
- 1 cup Gouda cheese, shredded
- Sour cream (for drizzling)
- Chives, chopped (for garnish)
- Salt and pepper to taste

Instructions:

Preheat your oven according to the pizza dough instructions.
Roll out the pizza dough on a floured surface to your desired thickness.
Spread a layer of diced cooked kopytka evenly over the pizza dough.
Distribute crumbled bacon and caramelized onions over the kopytka.
Sprinkle shredded Gouda cheese over the entire pizza.
Season with salt and pepper to taste.
Bake in the preheated oven until the crust is golden, and the cheese is melted and bubbly.
Remove from the oven and let it cool for a few minutes.
Drizzle sour cream over the hot pizza.
Garnish with chopped chives.
Slice and serve your Kopytka Kiss Pizza, a flavorful pizza inspired by Polish potato dumplings with bacon and Gouda cheese!

Polish Honey Cake Delight Pizza

Ingredients:

- Pizza dough
- 1/2 cup honey
- 1/4 cup unsalted butter, melted
- 1/2 cup sour cream
- 1/4 cup brown sugar
- 1 teaspoon ground cinnamon
- 1/2 teaspoon ground cloves
- 2 cups Graham cracker crumbs (for crust and topping)
- 1 cup whipped cream (for serving)
- Walnuts, chopped (for garnish)

Instructions:

Preheat your oven according to the pizza dough instructions.
Roll out the pizza dough on a floured surface to your desired thickness.
In a bowl, mix together honey, melted butter, sour cream, brown sugar, ground cinnamon, and ground cloves.
Spread a layer of the honey mixture over the pizza dough.
Sprinkle Graham cracker crumbs over the honey mixture, ensuring an even coating.
Bake in the preheated oven until the crust is golden and cooked through.
Remove from the oven and let it cool for a few minutes.
Drizzle more honey over the hot pizza.
Just before serving, top with a generous amount of whipped cream.
Sprinkle chopped walnuts over the whipped cream.
Slice and enjoy your Polish Honey Cake Delight Pizza, a sweet and indulgent twist on a classic Polish honey cake!

Golonka Gourmet Pizza

Ingredients:

- Pizza dough
- 1 cup cooked and shredded golonka (pork knuckle)
- 1/2 cup sauerkraut, drained and squeezed
- 1/4 cup whole grain mustard
- 1 cup Gruyère cheese, shredded
- Fresh parsley, chopped (for garnish)
- Salt and pepper to taste

Instructions:

Preheat your oven according to the pizza dough instructions.
Roll out the pizza dough on a floured surface to your desired thickness.
Spread a layer of whole grain mustard evenly over the pizza dough.
Distribute the cooked and shredded golonka (pork knuckle) over the mustard.
Scatter drained and squeezed sauerkraut over the golonka.
Sprinkle shredded Gruyère cheese over the entire pizza.
Season with salt and pepper to taste.
Bake in the preheated oven until the crust is golden, and the cheese is melted and bubbly.
Remove from the oven and let it cool for a few minutes.
Garnish with chopped fresh parsley.
Slice and serve your Golonka Gourmet Pizza, a delicious and hearty pizza inspired by the classic Polish dish of pork knuckle and sauerkraut!

Twarog Treat Pizza

Ingredients:

- Pizza dough
- 1 cup twaróg (Polish farmer's cheese), crumbled
- 1/4 cup honey
- 1/2 cup strawberries, sliced
- 1/4 cup blueberries
- 1/4 cup almonds, sliced
- Powdered sugar (for dusting)
- Mint leaves (for garnish)

Instructions:

Preheat your oven according to the pizza dough instructions.
Roll out the pizza dough on a floured surface to your desired thickness.
Spread the crumbled twaróg evenly over the pizza dough.
Drizzle honey over the twaróg, ensuring even coverage.
Arrange sliced strawberries, blueberries, and sliced almonds over the pizza.
Bake in the preheated oven until the crust is golden and cooked through.
Remove from the oven and let it cool for a few minutes.
Dust with powdered sugar for added sweetness.
Garnish with mint leaves.
Slice and serve your Twaróg Treat Pizza, a delightful and fruity dessert pizza featuring the richness of Polish farmer's cheese!

www.ingramcontent.com/pod-product-compliance
Lightning Source LLC
LaVergne TN
LVHW081343060526
838201LV00055B/2821